Journaling

Through

Grief

CONNIE BERG

WESTBOW
PRESS®
A DIVISION OF THOMAS NELSON
& ZONDERVAN

WestBow Press books may be ordered through booksellers or by contacting:

WestBow Press
A Division of Thomas Nelson & Zondervan
1663 Liberty Drive
Bloomington, IN 47403
www.westbowpress.com
844-714-3454

Scripture quotations taken from The Holy Bible, New International Version® NIV® Copyright © 1973 1978 1984 2011 by Biblica, Inc. TM. Used by permission. All rights reserved worldwide.

ISBN: 978-1-6642-5160-1 (sc)
ISBN: 978-1-6642-5161-8 (hc)
ISBN: 978-1-6642-5159-5 (e)

Library of Congress Control Number: 2021924444

Print information available on the last page.

WestBow Press rev. date: 12/21/2021

My sincerest thank you to Norm, Ben, Sarah, Gloria and Pastor Todd for your thoughts and advice which greatly helped to make this project worthy.

Dear friend,

I am so sorry for your loss. I truly am. My prayer for you is that you use this journal as a means of learning to cope with your loss and that you invite God to walk with you on your journey. His living and breathing Word will bring you much needed comfort in this time of sorrow.

Each page of this journal begins with a scripture and a reflection followed by a space to journal. Journal whatever comes to mind: your feelings, memories, or even a letter to your loved one. It is my hope and prayer that you end each entry with a prayer of your own.

Woven throughout the journal are pages encouraging you to write a letter to your loved one and other pages to place a photo and journal about a favorite memory. Writing a letter to your loved one has shown to be a positive activity toward healing.

Be gentle with yourself. Some days you will not feel like journaling; that's okay. There are no rules to grieving, but there are things we can do to cope in our grief, and journaling is a way of coping. On the days where we are in such agony all we can do is groan, the Holy Spirit intercedes on our behalf. God hears, and God heals.

Grief has no time line; it is different for everyone. When a loved one dies, many are left behind, and because everyone's relationship with that person was unique, each person's grief journey will be different. When my husband died, he left behind children, parents, siblings, and grandparents. While I pray you are able to grieve together with family and friends, it is important not to compare your grief. Making a competition of grief is not helpful and can be quite hurtful. But be prepared that this may happen, and my friend, be patient and forgiving knowing they are also in the midst of sorrow.

As you progress through the journal, be sure to go back and read past entries in order to give you encouragement as to how far you've come on your journey.

This is your journey. Use this journal as a safe place to bare your soul as you progress through the healing process. Treat it as your best friend as you pour your heart out on the pages within. I pray this journal speaks to your heart and brings strength for the day as you learn to cope with your loss.

Take heart,

Connie

To _____

From _____

May God Bless the Memory of:

_____

My prayer for you: _____

_____

_____

Forever in My Heart

Name _____

Birth _____

Death _____

[Jesus prayed] "Father, if you are willing, take this cup from me; yet not my will, but yours be done." (Luke 22:42)

It is normal to ask God to take away the accident or reverse the illness of your loved one; even Jesus asked that "this cup be taken from me." Oh, my friend, we don't know the reasons things happen as they do, but we know that God works for the good of all things for those who love Him and are called according to His purpose. At the time of Jesus' death, His followers saw only despair, yet we know that in Christ's death was our salvation. This was God's plan—and it was good. My prayer for you is that as you begin this journey you choose to trust and love God through your pain.

Date _____

_____

_____

_____

_____

_____

_____

_____

_____

_____

_____

_____

_____

_____

_____

_____

_____

_____

My prayer for today _____

_____

_____

For I am convinced that neither death nor life, neither angels nor demons, neither the present nor the future, nor any powers, neither height nor depth, nor anything else in all creation, will be able to separate us from the love of God that is in Christ Jesus our Lord. (Romans 8:38)

The only thing that can separate us from God is ourselves, no one and nothing else. Guilt is very real and a completely normal feeling following the death of a loved one. Try not to blame yourself for things that were never in your control. The accident happened. If you could have prevented it, you would have; it's not your fault. The illness took your loved one's last breath, it's not your fault. You weren't there when your loved one died, and you didn't get to say goodbye; it's not your fault. Guilt is self-punishment, and it steals away your feeling of self-worth. God loves you, He created you in His image, and, my friend, you are worthy! Continue to pray for God to remove any feelings of guilt so that you can begin the process of healing. Trust in the Lord, and ask Him to be by your side as a guide and as a friend as you start out on this most difficult journey.

Date _____

_____

_____

_____

_____

_____

_____

_____

_____

_____

_____

_____

_____

My prayer for today _____

_____

_____

Be still, and know that I am God. (Psalm 46:10)

Why, God, why! Why did you allow this to happen! In the midst of the anguish and despair of grief, you may not feel like turning to God for comfort because He allowed this to happen. It is normal to have moments of doubt, but in these moments, I pray you choose to love and trust God in all things. Be still and know that God loves you and has a plan for you. Ask Him into your heart, and allow Him to comfort you through this time.

Date _____

_____

_____

_____

_____

_____

_____

_____

_____

_____

_____

_____

_____

_____

_____

_____

_____

_____

My prayer for today _____

_____

_____

[Jesus said] "I have told you these things, so that in me you may have peace. In this world you will have trouble. But take heart! I have overcome the world." (John 16:33)

I clung to John 16:33 when my husband was diagnosed with ALS (amyotrophic lateral sclerosis). It gave me comfort to picture all the fragments of my shattered dreams being held in the palm of my Savior, Jesus Christ. I pray this vision brings you comfort as well.

Date _____

_____

_____

_____

_____

_____

_____

_____

_____

_____

_____

_____

_____

_____

_____

_____

_____

_____

_____

My prayer for today _____

_____

_____

[Jesus said] "So with you: Now is your time of grief, but I will see you again and you will rejoice, and no one will take away your joy." (John 16:22)

Take heart, my friend, in this beautiful promise. Jesus knows how deeply you are suffering, and He has compassion for you in this moment. Find assurance in His promise of eternal life, where there will be no more sorrow.

Date _____

_____
_____
_____
_____
_____
_____
_____
_____
_____
_____
_____
_____
_____
_____
_____
_____
_____
_____
_____
_____
_____
_____
_____
_____

My prayer for today _____
_____
_____

If it is possible, as far as it depends on you, live at peace with everyone.
(Romans 12:18)

As you share your grief with others, it is possible that some may start comparing their grief to yours. It is healthy to talk about your grief with one another and have compassion for each other, but take care not to compare your pain. When someone dies, there are many loved ones left behind. We all suffer in our own ways and in our own time frames. Our journeys are personal. Comparing your pain can be hurtful and unproductive. But, my friend, if this does happen, take a deep breath and choose grace.

Date _____

_____

_____

_____

_____

_____

_____

_____

_____

_____

_____

_____

_____

_____

_____

_____

_____

_____

My prayer for today _____

_____

_____

The Lord is righteous in all his ways and loving toward all he has made. The Lord is near to all who call on him, to all who call on him in truth. (Psalm 145:17–18)

Be honest with God about how you are feeling. Be honest with yourself also. Anger and depression are two very real stages of grief. So often we turn our anger toward God; try not to do this. Choose to come to Him in your pain, and ask Him to guide you through the seasons of grief. Self-destructive thoughts and behaviors are not part of the stages of grief. If you are experiencing these, seek professional help from a pastor or a grief counselor.

Date _____

_____

_____

_____

_____

_____

_____

_____

_____

_____

_____

_____

_____

_____

_____

_____

My prayer for today _____

_____

_____

Be merciful to me, Lord, for I am faint; O Lord, heal me, for my bones are in agony. My soul is in anguish. How long, O Lord, how long? (Psalm 6:2–3)

God knows your pain; He knows your hour of need. Saying goodbye to your loved one brings such agony and uncertainty. When my husband was dying, we said, "See you later," because we had faith our separation was for a time and not for forever. Take heart, my friend, you have your hope at the foot of the cross, and you will be reunited again one day.

Date _____

_____

_____

_____

_____

_____

_____

_____

_____

_____

_____

_____

_____

_____

_____

_____

_____

_____

_____

My prayer for today _____

_____

_____

How can we sing the songs of the Lord while in a foreign land? (Psalm 137:4)

Grieving the loss of a loved one throws us into the desert of despair. How is it possible to attain a grateful heart when in such pain? Give thanks for the time you had together. Give thanks for the memories you have. Give thanks for the person you are because of the time you shared together.

Date _____

_____

_____

_____

_____

_____

_____

_____

_____

_____

_____

_____

_____

_____

_____

_____

_____

_____

_____

My prayer for today _____

_____

_____

In the same way the Spirit helps us in our weakness. We do not know what we ought to pray for, but the Spirit himself intercedes for us with groans that words cannot express. And he who searches our hearts knows the mind of the Spirit, because the Spirit intercedes for the saints in accordance with God's will. (Romans 8:26)

Some days will be harder than others; some moments will seem unbearable. When your soul is in such agony, you can't hardly breathe, let alone find the words to pray, take heart in the invincible summer within you, the Holy Spirit. When there are no words, God hears your groans. He understands the depth of your pain, and He loves you through your tears.

Date _____

_____

_____

_____

_____

_____

_____

_____

_____

_____

_____

_____

_____

_____

_____

_____

_____

_____

My prayer for today _____

_____

_____

Write a letter to your loved one. Tell him or her about your day and how you feel. Or reminisce about a favorite memory.

Dear _____

_____
_____
_____
_____
_____
_____
_____
_____
_____
_____
_____
_____
_____
_____
_____
_____
_____
_____
_____
_____
_____
_____
_____
_____
_____
_____
_____

Turn to me and be gracious to me, for I am lonely and afflicted. (Psalm 25:16)

The funeral is past, the thank yous have been sent out, and family and friends have gone home. What now? Things are so quiet and lonely. Others go back to their normal lives, but yours has changed. There are no answers, no time lines. But we have the grace of God. Turn to Him, and allow Him to comfort you. Tell God your feelings and your fears; feel His love as you pour your heart out to Him.

Date _____

_____

_____

_____

_____

_____

_____

_____

_____

_____

_____

_____

_____

_____

_____

_____

_____

_____

_____

My prayer for today _____

_____

_____

Be merciful to me, O Lord, for I am in distress; my eyes grow weak with sorrow, my soul and my body with grief. My life is consumed by anguish and my years by groaning. (Psalm 31:9–10)

When you are overwhelmed by your grief, and all you can see and feel is the pain of loss, cry out to the Lord for His mercy. And be assured that as foreign as this new world seems to you, God is still in control. He's got you in the palm of His hand.

Date _____

_____

_____

_____

_____

_____

_____

_____

_____

_____

_____

_____

_____

_____

_____

_____

_____

_____

_____

_____

My prayer for today _____

_____

_____

The Lord is close to the brokenhearted and saves those who are crushed in spirit. (Psalm 34:18)

God created us in His image to love and have compassion for each other. He created love and compassion! Through Christ's salvation we have become the sons and daughters of God. As you write down your thoughts, feel the deep love of your Father as He comforts you in ways beyond our understanding.

Date _____

_____

_____

_____

_____

_____

_____

_____

_____

_____

_____

_____

_____

_____

_____

_____

_____

_____

_____

_____

My prayer for today _____

_____

_____

I am feeble and utterly crushed; I groan in anguish of heart. All my longings lie open before you, O Lord; my sighing is not hidden from you. (Psalm 38:8–9)

The Lord knows your pain. When your soul is desperately weary, when you can't sleep and your chest is so tight it hurts to breathe, take a long deep breath, blow it out slowly, and pray for comfort. Journal your feelings and use this as a safe place to bare your soul.

Date _____

_____

_____

_____

_____

_____

_____

_____

_____

_____

_____

_____

_____

_____

_____

_____

_____

_____

_____

My prayer for today _____

_____

_____

But you, O Lord, are a compassionate and gracious God, slow to anger, abounding in love and faithfulness. Turn to me and have mercy on me. (Psalm 86:15–16)

In moments of deep anguish, all we can do is cry out to the Lord, "Have mercy." He does hear our prayers. He doesn't instantly make the pain go away, but He does love us through our pain. When we come to God on our knees, we are made aware of our complete dependence on Him, and He helps us to grow.

Date _____

_____

_____

_____

_____

_____

_____

_____

_____

_____

_____

_____

_____

_____

_____

_____

_____

_____

_____

My prayer for today _____

_____

_____

I have suffered much; preserve my life, O Lord, according to your word. (Psalm 119:107)

While you are suffering the loss of a loved one, it is important to remember that others may be relying on you for various reasons. When my husband died, I had three teenagers. Three very angry teenagers questioning why their dad died. I was suffering, but I needed the Lord to preserve my life so I could raise my children. Take care of yourself, and be gentle with yourself. Others are depending on you.

Date _____

_____

_____

_____

_____

_____

_____

_____

_____

_____

_____

_____

_____

_____

_____

_____

_____

_____

My prayer for today _____

_____

_____

Out of the depths I cry to you, O Lord; O Lord, hear my voice. Let your ears be attentive to my cry for mercy. (Psalm 130:1–2)

There are some days and moments when the anguish is so great you may not feel God's presence through your tears. In these moments take that leap of faith, and know that God is with you. Write out one of your favorite Bible verses and tape it to your bathroom mirror as a constant reminder the Lord is near.

Date _____

_____

_____

_____

_____

_____

_____

_____

_____

_____

_____

_____

_____

_____

_____

_____

_____

_____

My prayer for today _____

_____

_____

The Lord is gracious and compassionate, slow to anger and rich in love. The Lord is good to all; he has compassion on all he has made. (Psalm 145:8–9)

Our God is loving and compassionate. He takes no pleasure in your pain; He is loving you through the storm and will guide you to the other side. The storm cannot be avoided or skirted around. You have to go through it to get to the other side. Take heart; God is with you and lighting your path to the other side.

Date _____

_____

_____

_____

_____

_____

_____

_____

_____

_____

_____

_____

_____

_____

_____

_____

_____

_____

_____

_____

My prayer for today _____

_____

_____

My soul yearns for you in the night; in the morning my spirit longs for you.
(Isaiah 26:9)

There is an emptiness in our hearts when we lose loved ones. The emptiness will always be filled with something over time, but not all things will make you whole again. Choose God and His love to fill the emptiness and make you whole.

Date _____

_____

_____

_____

_____

_____

_____

_____

_____

_____

_____

_____

_____

_____

_____

_____

_____

_____

_____

_____

_____

_____

My prayer for today _____

_____

_____

I will refresh the weary and satisfy the faint. (Jeremiah 31:25)

Grief takes energy. Oh, so much energy! For now, you may feel weary and faint but know that this is only for a time. The tears will still come, but they will come less frequently over time as God restores you. He will help you learn to cope with your loss.

Date _____

_____

_____

_____

_____

_____

_____

_____

_____

_____

_____

_____

_____

_____

_____

_____

_____

_____

_____

_____

_____

_____

My prayer for today _____

_____

_____

Treasured Memory

I called on your name, O Lord, from the depths of the pit. You heard my plea: "Do not close your ears to my cry for relief." You came near when I called you, and you said, "Do not fear." (Lamentations 3:55–57)

When my husband died, I felt incredibly lonely and empty, as though I was in an abyss of anguish. Friends wanted to support me, but they didn't know how. And I wasn't able to articulate my needs. Call on the Lord, my friend. He hears you, He knows your needs, and He will provide the manna needed for the day.

Date _____

_____

_____

_____

_____

_____

_____

_____

_____

_____

_____

_____

_____

_____

_____

My prayer for today _____

_____

_____

I can do everything through him who gives me strength. (Philippians 4:13)

A phrase that is often said to those who are grieving is, "God doesn't give you more than you can handle." Nothing could be further from the truth. That statement is nowhere in the Bible, and it can be so hurtful to hear those words implying if you weren't so strong, this wouldn't have happened. God didn't give you this loss because you could handle it. You can handle this loss because He gives you the much-needed strength to endure.

Date _____

_____

_____

_____

_____

_____

_____

_____

_____

_____

_____

_____

_____

_____

_____

_____

_____

_____

_____

My prayer for today _____

_____

_____

I cry out to you, O God, but you do not answer. (Job 30:20)

You've perhaps prayed for a cure to an illness or a miracle to reverse the tragedy, and God doesn't seem to hear. He does hear, my friend, and He does love you. But sometimes the answer is no for reasons we cannot possibly understand. Trust that He loves you and that He mourns with you. Trust there will be sunshine in your life again one day, and you will know His peace.

Date _____

_____

_____

_____

_____

_____

_____

_____

_____

_____

_____

_____

_____

_____

_____

_____

_____

_____

_____

My prayer for today _____

_____

_____

The Lord is a refuge for the oppressed, a stronghold in times of trouble.
(Psalm 9:9)

One of the hardest lessons to accept in life is that we are not in control. There is an old Swedish proverb that states, "The afternoon knows what the morning never suspected." Isn't that the truth! In this painful time, as you choose to turn toward God in faith and hope, may you know His peace and feel His presence as you surrender to Him on this most difficult journey.

Date _____

_____

_____

_____

_____

_____

_____

_____

_____

_____

_____

_____

_____

_____

_____

_____

_____

_____

_____

My prayer for today _____

_____

_____

Bear with each other and forgive whatever grievances you may have against one another. Forgive as the Lord forgave you. (Colossians 3:13)

Sometimes people say hurtful things when trying to offer consolations. When my husband died, a woman said she knew how I felt because her cat had just died. I'm sure she was attached to her cat, but I failed to see the comparison at the time. Over time I began to realize the worst storm is the one we are in. She was lonely and grieving the loss of her cat. When people say something shocking or hurtful, take a deep breath and choose grace.

Date _____

My prayer for today _____

But as for me and my household, we will serve the Lord. (Joshua 24:15)

The feelings of anger and unfairness can at times eclipse our feelings of trust and faith in a God that allows such pain. How can I trust God when He allowed my loved one to die? Why did He allow it? It is in these moments I pray you choose to trust God and know with confidence that you will one day be reunited with your loved one, and there will be no more tears in heaven.

Date _____

_____

_____

_____

_____

_____

_____

_____

_____

_____

_____

_____

_____

_____

_____

_____

_____

_____

_____

My prayer for today _____

_____

_____

Surely, O God, you have worn me out; you have devastated my entire household. Even now my witness is in heaven; my advocate is on high. My intercessor is my friend as my eyes pour out tears to God. (Job 16:7, 19–21)

God doesn't cause all our suffering, although the devil would love it if we thought He did. But God does allow pain and suffering. We are human, and when we allow ourselves to love, we open ourselves to loss. God blessed you with a loving relationship and gave you the gift of memory to remember your loved one. With the hope that is in the cross, be assured that this separation from your loved one is for a season, not forever.

Date _____

_____

_____

_____

_____

_____

_____

_____

_____

_____

_____

_____

_____

_____

_____

_____

_____

_____

_____

My prayer for today _____

_____

_____

To you, O Lord, I lift up my soul; in you I trust, O my God. No one whose hope is in you will ever be put to shame. Show me your ways, O Lord, teach me your paths; guide me in your truth and teach me, for you are God my Savior, and my hope is in you all day long. (Psalm 25:1, 3, 5)

Your world is changed; the future you anticipated can no longer be. Seek the Lord, and ask Him to guide you through this painful time of adjusting to a new and unplanned for future. Your hope in the Lord will not be put to shame as He strengthens you and leads you to a future that once again knows joy.

Date _____

_____

_____

_____

_____

_____

_____

_____

_____

_____

_____

_____

_____

_____

_____

_____

_____

_____

_____

_____

My prayer for today _____

_____

_____

My heart is blighted and withered like grass; I forget to eat my food. Because of my loud groaning I am reduced to skin and bones. (Psalm 102:4–5)

Turn to God for comfort and strength in your darkest hour. We know the seasons change, and with every winter we have confidence spring will follow. Just as assuredly, in the depth of the winter of your soul, springtime will follow, and you will have joy again.

Date _____

_____

_____

_____

_____

_____

_____

_____

_____

_____

_____

_____

_____

_____

_____

_____

_____

_____

_____

_____

My prayer for today _____

_____

_____

But I trust in you, O Lord; I say, "You are my God." My times are in your hands. Let your face shine on your servant; save me in your unfailing love. (Psalm 31:14–16)

God doesn't stop the rain from falling or disease or accidents from happening. In the midst of this storm, can you find hope in knowing that all the seasons of your life are in His hands? In Isaiah 44:2 (CEV), God proclaims, "I am your creator. You were in my care even before you were born." I pray you find comfort in knowing that our Creator is holding you in His care and that you have been in His care even before you were born.

Date _____

_____

_____

_____

_____

_____

_____

_____

_____

_____

_____

_____

_____

_____

_____

_____

_____

_____

My prayer for today _____

_____

_____

Write a letter to your loved one. Tell him or her about your day and how you feel. Or reminisce about a favorite memory.

Dear _____

_____

_____

_____

_____

_____

_____

_____

_____

_____

_____

_____

_____

_____

_____

_____

_____

_____

_____

_____

_____

_____

_____

_____

_____

_____

_____

_____

My soul is weary with sorrow; strengthen me according to your word. (Psalm 119:28)

It is through God's living Word that we find solace from the storm and strength to face the day. Spend time reading the book of Psalms written so long ago, and find the timeless providence of God woven within. May this bring you peace in the moment and hope for the future.

Date _____

_____

_____

_____

_____

_____

_____

_____

_____

_____

_____

_____

_____

_____

_____

_____

_____

_____

My prayer for today _____

_____

_____

I will not forget you! See, I have engraved you on the palms of my hands.
(Isaiah 49:15–16)

God has not forgotten you and will never forsake you. Your suffering is very real, but know that God is with you, and you will one day be restored as He gives you the strength to cope with your loss. With that perspective can you find the joy of loving God, your Father, through your tears?

Date _____

_____

_____

_____

_____

_____

_____

_____

_____

_____

_____

_____

_____

_____

_____

_____

_____

_____

My prayer for today _____

_____

_____

"Though the mountains be shaken and the hills be removed, yet my unfailing love for you will not be shaken nor my covenant of peace be removed," says the Lord, who has compassion on you. (Isaiah 54:10)

When your world has been changed, your plans upended, and you can't begin to make sense of a future without your loved one, take heart. The Lord's love is unfailing. May His peace that passes all understanding fill your heart and soul.

Date _____

_____

_____

_____

_____

_____

_____

_____

_____

_____

_____

_____

_____

_____

_____

_____

_____

_____

_____

_____

My prayer for today _____

_____

_____

"For I know the plans I have for you," declares the Lord, "plans to prosper you and not to harm you, plans to give you hope and a future." (Jeremiah 29:11)

God is not cruel and does not take pleasure in our suffering. Christ suffered greatly during the Passion, yet it was in His victory over death that we have our hope in salvation. Suffering doesn't make sense, and it seems so unfair. Yet it is part of this fallen world in which we live. Trust your Father as He holds your future in the palm of His hand.

Date _____

_____

_____

_____

_____

_____

_____

_____

_____

_____

_____

_____

_____

_____

_____

_____

_____

_____

_____

My prayer for today _____

_____

_____

In my distress I called to the Lord and he answered me. (Jonah 2:2)

God talks to us in many ways; we just need a willing spirit to hear Him. Listen for Him in the laughter of a child, look for Him in the beauty of a sunrise, and feel His presence in the embrace of a friend.

Date _____

_____

_____

_____

_____

_____

_____

_____

_____

_____

_____

_____

_____

_____

_____

_____

_____

_____

_____

_____

_____

My prayer for today _____

_____

_____

But as for me, I watch in hope for the Lord, I wait for God my Savior; my God will hear me. (Micah 7:7)

On the lonely nights when you can't sleep and your heart aches for your loved one, let the tears fall. And through the tears call out to the Lord and know He draws near as you put your hope in Him.

Date _____

_____

_____

_____

_____

_____

_____

_____

_____

_____

_____

_____

_____

_____

_____

_____

_____

_____

_____

_____

My prayer for today _____

_____

_____

[Mary said] "Lord, if you had been here, my brother would not have died."
When Jesus saw her weeping, and those that had come along with her
also weeping, he was deeply moved in spirit and troubled. (John 11:32–33)

Separation through death is agonizing and would be hopeless if it were
not for the hope we have in the cross. God cares so much for us that He
sent His only Son, Jesus Christ, to die on the cross for our sins so that we
would have eternal life. He does allow death and the pain we suffer from
that loss, but my friend, He knows your pain. He has literally felt your
pain, and He has compassion for you.

Date _____

_____

_____

_____

_____

_____

_____

_____

_____

_____

_____

_____

_____

_____

_____

_____

_____

_____

My prayer for today _____

_____

_____

You are my lamp, O Lord; the Lord turns my darkness into light. (2 Samuel 22:29)

The lighthouse has long been a symbol of God's light guiding us through our storms to calmer waters. I pray you trust Him as He guides you on this journey. Memory is such a gift, and thanks be to God, you will remember your loved one. My son was terrified he would forget what his dad looked like. He cried in agony one day, "I can't see his face!" It is in the memories we can still see their face, hear their voice, and feel their touch. Cherish your memories and write them down.

Date _____

_____

_____

_____

_____

_____

_____

_____

_____

_____

_____

_____

_____

_____

_____

_____

_____

_____

My prayer for today _____

_____

_____

And God said, "This is the sign of the covenant I am making between me and you and every living creature with you, a covenant for all generations to come: I have set my rainbow in the clouds, and it will be the sign of the covenant between me and the earth." (Genesis 9:12–13)

I love rainbows, not only for their beauty, but also for the hope they bring after a storm. When God allows pain to enter our lives, it's really hard to trust in Him. Life isn't always fair. I'll never understand why God allowed my husband to suffer and die from ALS. But I do believe in God, my Father, and I choose to trust Him to work good in all things. I'm sure the evening of Christ's crucifixion the disciples were confused and in shock as to why God would allow such a tragic death. But it is through Christ's death on the cross that we have our salvation. When things don't make sense and life isn't fair, choose to see the promise in the rainbow.

Date _____

_____

_____

_____

_____

_____

_____

_____

_____

_____

_____

_____

_____

_____

_____

My prayer for today _____

_____

_____

If it is possible, as far as it depends on you, live at peace with everyone. (Romans 12:18)

A friend recently buried her husband. This was his second marriage following the death of his first wife. His children never accepted this second marriage and treated their stepmother with contempt. This selfish behavior was extremely hurtful and destroyed relationships. My friend is a true daughter of Christ, and despite the harsh treatment, she made sure the funeral was focused on his children because, she said, "They were in his life first." Such grace! We cannot control others, but we can control how we respond to others, and we can choose to respond with grace.

Date _____

_____

_____

_____

_____

_____

_____

_____

_____

_____

_____

_____

_____

_____

_____

_____

_____

My prayer for today _____

_____

_____

Treasured Memory

For the Lamb at the center of the throne will be their shepherd; he will lead them to springs of living water. And God will wipe away every tear from their eyes. (Revelation 7:17)

No more tears in heaven! Can you even imagine the new kingdom? We were not created for this world. Is it possible in this time of pain and questioning to thank the Lord for giving us the message that a new age will come, and to be thankful that the tears of today will not be in the new kingdom? Amen. Come, Lord Jesus!

Date _____

_____

_____

_____

_____

_____

_____

_____

_____

_____

_____

_____

_____

_____

_____

_____

_____

My prayer for today _____

_____

_____

When anxiety was great within me, your consolation brought joy to my soul.
(Psalm 94:19)

Turn to the Lord in prayer, and turn to His Word for comfort. Especially find comfort in the book of Psalms. King David had great tribulation, but he recognized he also had joy in the Lord. Seek joy in the Lord.

Date _____

_____

_____

_____

_____

_____

_____

_____

_____

_____

_____

_____

_____

_____

_____

_____

_____

_____

_____

My prayer for today _____

_____

_____

The Lord your God is with you, he is mighty to save. (Zephaniah 3:17)

Ponder this verse. Our Father, Creator of the heavens, the earth, and all that exists; who is infinite in time and space, who is all-knowing, ever-present and unlimited in power; our Father, who IS love, loves you, and in His compassion is mightily saving you.

Date _____

_____

_____

_____

_____

_____

_____

_____

_____

_____

_____

_____

_____

_____

_____

_____

_____

_____

_____

_____

_____

My prayer for today _____

_____

_____

Because of the Lord's great love we are not consumed, for his compassions never fail. They are new every morning; great is your faithfulness. I say to myself, "The Lord is my portion: therefore I will wait for him." The Lord is good to those whose hope is in him, to the one who seeks him; it is good to wait quietly for the salvation of the Lord. (Lamentations 3:22–26)

As the manna was new every morning for the Jews as they wandered forty years in the desert, so our Father sends His manna to you each morning, manna in the form of a caring friend, a kind word from a stranger, encouragement in a whisper.

Date _____

_____

_____

_____

_____

_____

_____

_____

_____

_____

_____

_____

_____

_____

_____

_____

_____

_____

My prayer for today _____

_____

_____

We live by faith, not by sight. (2 Corinthians 5:7)

There is no road map to grief. Everyone grieves in their own way and in their own time. What works for some may not work for you, and vice versa. In this moment come to the Lord in faith, and ask your Father to guide your steps on this journey.

Date _____

_____

_____

_____

_____

_____

_____

_____

_____

_____

_____

_____

_____

_____

_____

_____

_____

_____

_____

_____

My prayer for today _____

_____

_____

Do not be anxious about anything, but in everything, by prayer and petition, with thanksgiving, present your requests to God. And the peace of God, which transcends all understanding, will guard your hearts and your minds in Christ Jesus. (Philippians 4:6–7)

Through your tears turn to God with a thankful heart for having been blessed to spend the time you had with your loved one. Ask Him to calm any anxiety, strengthen you with His love, and grant you His peace as you continue on this journey.

Date _____

_____

_____

_____

_____

_____

_____

_____

_____

_____

_____

_____

_____

_____

_____

_____

_____

_____

My prayer for today _____

_____

_____

God has said, "Never will I leave you; never will I forsake you." So we say with confidence, "The Lord is my helper; I will not be afraid." (Hebrews 13:5–6)

God does allow painful things to happen, but while we may not know His reasons, we can be assured that He will be with us in all things and comfort us through all things so that through Him, we can endure all things.

Date _____

_____

_____

_____

_____

_____

_____

_____

_____

_____

_____

_____

_____

_____

_____

_____

_____

_____

My prayer for today _____

_____

_____

How great is the love the Father has lavished on us, that we should be called children of God! (1 John 3:1)

And that is what we are! You know the love you have for your family and closest friends; you would do almost anything for them. God's love is greater than anything you or I can possibly comprehend. We are His children! Trust that He will comfort you and provide for you.

Date _____

_____

_____

_____

_____

_____

_____

_____

_____

_____

_____

_____

_____

_____

_____

_____

_____

_____

My prayer for today _____

_____

_____

A truthful witness gives honest testimony. (Proverbs 12:17)

I've always considered "fine" a four-letter F word. After my house fire, people would ask, "How are you doing?" I always said, "Fine." Which wasn't true at all. When emotions are raw, it's very difficult to share those feelings honestly with others. Sometimes we can't even articulate those feelings. God brings people into our lives for such moments as these. Sharing your feelings with a close friend or a pastor can be very healing. Also, this journal is a trusted friend with which you can bare your soul.

Date _____

_____

_____

_____

_____

_____

_____

_____

_____

_____

_____

_____

_____

_____

_____

_____

_____

_____

_____

My prayer for today _____

_____

_____

One day Jesus said to his disciples, "Let's go over to the other side of the lake." So they got into a boat and set out. As they sailed, he fell asleep. A squall came down on the lake, so that the boat was being swamped, and they were in great danger. The disciples went and woke him saying, "Master, Master we're going to drown!" He got up and rebuked the wind and the raging waters; the storm subsided, and all was calm. "Where is your faith?" he asked his disciples. (Luke 8:22–25)

Jesus calms the storms in our daily struggles as we learn to cope with the loss of our loved ones. The storms of anger, anguish, loneliness, crying to the point where there are no tears left. When one day at a time is too much, take things moment by moment. Take a deep breath, let it out slowly, and remember Jesus is in the boat with you. Look to Him for the peace that only He can provide in the midst of your suffering.

Date _____

_____

_____

_____

_____

_____

_____

_____

_____

_____

_____

_____

_____

_____

_____

My prayer for today _____

_____

_____

Write a letter to your loved one. Tell him or her about your day and how you feel. Or reminisce about a favorite memory.

Dear _____

The Lord bless you and keep you; the Lord make his face shine upon you and be gracious to you; the Lord turn his face toward you and give you peace. (Numbers 6:24–26)

Loss of a loved one creates such pain and loneliness in many ways. When I lost my spouse, I was now alone to raise our children, often wondering how he would have handled certain situations. But I also wasn't able to do things couples do, such as going out to movies or out for dinner. When you are feeling alone and isolated, I pray you feel God's presence and His peace through your tears.

Date _____

_____
_____
_____
_____
_____
_____
_____
_____
_____
_____
_____
_____
_____
_____
_____
_____

My prayer for today _____
_____
_____

The Lord is my rock, my fortress and my deliverer; my God is my rock in whom I take refuge, my shield and the horn of my salvation. He is my stronghold, my refuge and my savior. (2 Samuel 22:2–3)

Grief is a necessary journey one has to take in order to emerge whole again. It can't be avoided, and while some will come along our paths to support us, they can't take the journey for us. Some people are tempted to help sea turtle nestlings as they emerge from their shells and make the dangerous journey across the sand to the ocean. The journey is difficult, but in their struggles, their flippers gain the strength needed to survive life in the ocean. May you be mindful of the hope you have in the cross of Christ as your "flippers" gain strength on your journey to healing, my friend.

Date _____

_____

_____

_____

_____

_____

_____

_____

_____

_____

_____

_____

_____

_____

_____

My prayer for today _____

_____

_____

To God belong wisdom and power; counsel and understanding are his. (Job 12:13)

God is our all-knowing and loving Father. He knows exactly what you're feeling, so be honest with Him and with yourself. In order to have true healing, you need God's counsel to cope with your pain and heal your heart. Write down your feelings, and trust in His wisdom to counsel you through this storm to a renewed heart filled with praise and thanksgiving. Praise for His gift of salvation and thanksgiving for the blessing of the time you had with your loved one.

Date _____

_____

_____

_____

_____

_____

_____

_____

_____

_____

_____

_____

_____

_____

_____

_____

_____

_____

_____

My prayer for today _____

_____

_____

The Lord is my shepherd, I shall not be in want. He makes me lie down in green pastures, he leads me beside quiet waters, he restores my soul. He guides me in paths of righteousness for his name's sake. Even though I walk through the valley of the shadow of death, I will fear no evil, for you are with me; your rod and your staff, they comfort me. You prepare a table before me in the presence of my enemies. You anoint my head with oil; my cup overflows. Surely goodness and love will follow me all the days of my life, and I will dwell in the house of the Lord forever. (Psalm 23)

These verses are read at many Christian funerals, but do you know the depth of what they mean? We have no control over death; we are helpless. We may be able to show courage in times of testing or trial, but death is out of our reach. We take solace with the knowledge that God has conquered death, and He will welcome us one day to be with Him in the life everlasting.

Date _____

_____

_____

_____

_____

_____

_____

_____

_____

_____

_____

_____

_____

_____

My prayer for today _____

_____

_____

The Lord has heard my cry for mercy; the Lord accepts my prayer. (Psalm 6:9)

Be assured, my friend, the Lord has heard your prayers, and He is loving you through this. One of the benefits of journaling is that you can go back and read earlier entries. On days you feel stuck, go back, and be assured of the progress you've made and know that God is answering your cry for mercy.

Date _____

_____
_____
_____
_____
_____
_____
_____
_____
_____
_____
_____
_____
_____
_____
_____
_____
_____
_____
_____
_____
_____

My prayer for today _____

_____
_____

Where, O death, is your victory? Where, O death, is your sting? The sting of death is sin, and the power of sin is the law. But thanks be to God! He gives us the victory through our Lord Jesus Christ. (1 Corinthians 15:55–57)

God does not remove the storms from our lives, but it is in these storms we come to Him on our knees in complete surrender to His grace and give thanks for the hope we have in the gift of salvation. The only thing we have to do to receive this amazing gift is to believe in Jesus Christ. In Christ, death is temporary; in Christ, we all will be raised up to live eternally in the awesome presence of God our Father. Amen!

Date _____

_____

_____

_____

_____

_____

_____

_____

_____

_____

_____

_____

_____

_____

_____

_____

My prayer for today _____

_____

_____

In the midst of winter I found there was within me an invincible summer.

—Albert Camus

While I don't believe this is what Camus had in mind, this quote reminds me of the Holy Spirit within me, and He makes my soul invincible. Give thanks and praise the Lord for placing the Holy Spirit within you and giving you an invincible summer!

Date _____

_____

_____

_____

_____

_____

_____

_____

_____

_____

_____

_____

_____

_____

_____

_____

_____

My prayer for today _____

_____

_____

Praise be to the Lord, for he has heard my cry for mercy. The lord is my strength and my shield; my heart trusts in him, and I am helped. (Psalm 28:6–7)

Our God of compassion hears your cries for mercy. Trust in Him to uplift your spirit as you continue on this journey of grief. As you choose to trust in God, tell Him a memory you shared with your loved one, and give thanks for the blessing of that moment.

Date _____

_____

_____

_____

_____

_____

_____

_____

_____

_____

_____

_____

_____

_____

_____

_____

_____

_____

My prayer for today _____

_____

_____

Everyone should be quick to listen, slow to speak and slow to become angry, for man's anger does not bring about the righteous life that God desires. (James 1:19–20)

Especially in our deepest sorrow, God has compassion for us and loves us. One of the stages of grief is anger. God understands our humanity, but don't get stuck in your anger because that can lead to destruction and become a roadblock to your healing. Turn to God, ask Him to shield you from anger or bitterness, and trust Him to love you through your tears.

Date _____

_____

_____

_____

_____

_____

_____

_____

_____

_____

_____

_____

_____

_____

_____

_____

_____

_____

My prayer for today _____

_____

_____

My soul finds rest in God alone; my salvation comes from him. He alone is my rock and my salvation; he is my fortress, I will never be shaken. (Psalm 62:1–2)

Family and friends are much-needed support, but they are human; they can't possibly know our every need. When we're grieving, there are times we can't even articulate our needs. But God knows our every need; trust Him to be your rock and salvation in those moments.

Date _____

_____

_____

_____

_____

_____

_____

_____

_____

_____

_____

_____

_____

_____

_____

_____

_____

_____

My prayer for today _____

_____

_____

Treasured Memory

O my Strength, I watch for you; you, O God, are my fortress, my loving God. (Psalm 59:9)

Philippians 4:13 tells us we can do all things through Him who gives us strength. I would say it is also true that we cannot get through most things—especially grief—without our God. Draw your strength in and from the Lord with the hope you have at the foot of the cross.

Date _____

_____
_____
_____
_____
_____
_____
_____
_____
_____
_____
_____
_____
_____
_____
_____
_____
_____
_____
_____

My prayer for today _____

_____
_____

But those who hope in the Lord will renew their strength. They will soar on wings like eagles; they will run and not grow weary, they will walk and not be faint. (Isaiah 40:31)

This is God's promise to you. Do take His advice, and put your hope and trust in Him. In the Bible God tells us we will have times of joy but also times of trial. He doesn't sugarcoat it. But He does promise He will raise us to new heights, and we will have joy once again. Imagine the joy of soaring on eagles wings!

Date _____

_____
_____
_____
_____
_____
_____
_____
_____
_____
_____
_____
_____
_____
_____
_____
_____
_____

My prayer for today _____

_____
_____

Your sun will never set again, and your moon will wane no more; the Lord will be your everlasting light, and your days of sorrow will end. (Isaiah 60:20)

In this fallen world in which we live there are times we have to endure great pain. Through the tears and anguish remember this life is for a time, but in God's timing, one day you will have a new life in heaven, and there will be no more sorrow.

Date _____

_____

_____

_____

_____

_____

_____

_____

_____

_____

_____

_____

_____

_____

_____

_____

_____

_____

_____

_____

_____

My prayer for today _____

_____

_____

[Jesus said] "I am the resurrection and the life. He who believes in me will live, even though he dies; and whoever lives and believes in me will never die." (John 11:25)

What a beautiful comforting truth! Your loved one has left this physical world, and the pain of that separation is very real. But take heart because your pain and separation are also temporary. In Christ's resurrection and in this promise you have your hope.

Date _____

_____

_____

_____

_____

_____

_____

_____

_____

_____

_____

_____

_____

_____

_____

_____

_____

_____

My prayer for today _____

_____

_____

[Jesus said] "Peace I leave with you; my peace I give you. I do not give to you as the world gives. Do not let your hearts be troubled and do not be afraid." (John 14:27)

God's peace is so great it is impossible for us to comprehend. His peace is not absence of pain in our lives, but it is peace in His assurance that in any circumstance, we can do all things through Him who gives us strength.

Date _____

_____

_____

_____

_____

_____

_____

_____

_____

_____

_____

_____

_____

_____

_____

_____

_____

_____

_____

_____

My prayer for today _____

_____

_____

I waited patiently for the Lord; he turned to me and heard my cry. (Psalm 40:1)

Patience is not one of my strong suits. But as I reflect on my experiences, I do see how the Lord has provided for me through a kind visit from a friend or words of encouragement from a stranger. Remembering His grace in times of trial leads to patience as we wait on the Lord.

Date _____

_____

_____

_____

_____

_____

_____

_____

_____

_____

_____

_____

_____

_____

_____

_____

_____

_____

_____

_____

My prayer for today _____

_____

_____

Weeping may remain for a night, but rejoicing comes in the morning. (Psalm 30:5)

The nights were always the hardest for me. Everything was so quiet, and I could only think of how much I missed my husband by my side. In the loneliest of moments, trust that God is with you, and He is holding you in the palm of His hand.

Date _____

_____

_____

_____

_____

_____

_____

_____

_____

_____

_____

_____

_____

_____

_____

_____

_____

_____

My prayer for today _____

_____

_____

The Spirit of God has made me; the breath of the Almighty gives me life.
(Job 33:4)

I love the thought of God breathing life into us. Each day we need His breath to renew our spirits. Be in God's Word, and allow Him to breathe new life into you each day and refresh your spirit.

Date _____

_____

_____

_____

_____

_____

_____

_____

_____

_____

_____

_____

_____

_____

_____

_____

_____

_____

_____

_____

_____

My prayer for today _____

_____

_____

But God will not forget the needy; the hope of the afflicted will never perish. (Psalm 9:18)

Our hope lies at the foot of the cross in the salvation offered by Jesus Christ. You are separated for a time from your loved one, but take heart. You will be reunited one day.

Date _____

_____

_____

_____

_____

_____

_____

_____

_____

_____

_____

_____

_____

_____

_____

_____

_____

_____

_____

_____

My prayer for today _____

_____

_____

I am still confident of this: I will see the goodness of the Lord in the land of the living. Wait for the Lord; be strong and take heart and wait for the Lord. (Psalm 27:14)

What a gift the Word of God is. There are many different religions, but Christianity is the only one where our God came into our world to testify to His truth. God in all His glory comes to us in our hours of need and meets us where we are at. Trust in the truth of God's Word and know He loves you.

Date _____

_____

_____

_____

_____

_____

_____

_____

_____

_____

_____

_____

_____

_____

_____

_____

_____

_____

My prayer for today _____

_____

_____

Write a letter to your loved one. Tell him or her about your day and how you feel. Or reminisce about a favorite memory.

Dear _____

_____

_____

_____

_____

_____

_____

_____

_____

_____

_____

_____

_____

_____

_____

_____

_____

_____

_____

_____

_____

_____

_____

_____

_____

_____

_____

_____

And we know that in all things God works for the good of those who love him, who have been called according to his purpose. (Romans 8:28)

When nothing makes sense at this time, and it seems as though nothing good could possibly come from the death of your loved one, try to have faith in this promise. Bad things happen, and we have no control over them. But God does, and His ways are not the ways of this world. When He promises to work for your good in all things, He means it. Trust Him to do a good work in you.

Date _____

_____
_____
_____
_____
_____
_____
_____
_____
_____
_____
_____
_____
_____
_____
_____
_____
_____
_____

My prayer for today _____
_____
_____

I lift my eyes to the hills—where does my help come from? My help comes from the Lord, the Maker of heaven and earth. (Psalm 121:1–2)

God promises He will never leave us or forsake us. Our God, who is the Creator of all creation, comes to us in our pain and strengthens us through His love. Look to Him for strength for the day and peace in the moment.

Date _____

_____

_____

_____

_____

_____

_____

_____

_____

_____

_____

_____

_____

_____

_____

_____

_____

_____

_____

_____

My prayer for today _____

_____

_____

He heals the brokenhearted and binds up their wounds. He determines the number of the stars and calls them each by name. Great is our Lord and mighty in power; his understanding has no limit. (Psalm 147:3–5)

It's incredible that our God—who created the heavens and the earth, who determines the number of stars—comes close to us and heals our broken hearts. He is close to you right now, in this moment. Talk to Him, and let Him know how you feel.

Date _____

_____

_____

_____

_____

_____

_____

_____

_____

_____

_____

_____

_____

_____

_____

_____

_____

_____

My prayer for today _____

_____

_____

O Lord, be gracious to us; we long for you. Be our strength every morning, our salvation in time of distress. (Isaiah 33:2)

Seek the Lord in the morning and throughout your day. When our eyes are opened to the Lord, it's amazing how we can see that He does reach out to us. Don't ignore the miracles and dismiss them as coincidences or nothing at all. Choose to see the miracle. A visit from a friend or a kind word at just the right moment is God pouring His love out on you.

Date _____

_____

_____

_____

_____

_____

_____

_____

_____

_____

_____

_____

_____

_____

_____

_____

_____

_____

My prayer for today _____

_____

_____

Though he brings grief, he will show compassion, so great is his unfailing love. For he does not willingly bring affliction or grief to the children of men. (Lamentations 3:32–33)

It rains on the just and the unjust; pain and suffering come to everyone. But God promises us strength for the day, compassion in the moment, and hope for the future.

Date _____

_____
_____
_____
_____
_____
_____
_____
_____
_____
_____
_____
_____
_____
_____
_____
_____
_____
_____

My prayer for today _____
_____
_____

Come to me, all you who are weary and burdened, and I will give you rest ... for I am gentle and humble in heart, and you will find rest for your souls. (Matthew 11:28)

Jesus doesn't say, "I will take away your loss." In fact, throughout the Bible it is made very clear that we will at times have trouble. We live in a fallen world, and with that brings suffering. But we know that our God is gentle and humble in heart, and we look to Him for comfort.

Date _____

_____

_____

_____

_____

_____

_____

_____

_____

_____

_____

_____

_____

_____

_____

_____

_____

My prayer for today _____

_____

_____

Be joyful in hope, patient in affliction, faithful in prayer. (Romans 12:12)

Not joyful in grief but joyful in hope while we are grieving. Joyful in our hope in salvation through Jesus Christ. Patient in affliction because we know this life is temporary. Faithful in prayer, humbly acknowledging our dependence on God and coming before Him in complete surrender.

Date _____

_____

_____

_____

_____

_____

_____

_____

_____

_____

_____

_____

_____

_____

_____

_____

_____

_____

_____

_____

My prayer for today _____

_____

_____

Now faith is being sure of what we hope for and certain of what we do not see. (Hebrews 11:1)

We are sure in our hope of salvation because people witnessed the death and resurrection of Jesus Christ, and their God-inspired accounts are in the New Testament. We are certain of what we do not see because we have the Word of God and the Holy Spirit within. Amen!

Date _____

_____

_____

_____

_____

_____

_____

_____

_____

_____

_____

_____

_____

_____

_____

_____

_____

_____

_____

_____

My prayer for today _____

_____

_____

In the morning, O Lord, you hear my voice; in the morning I lay my requests before you and wait in expectation. (Psalm 5:3)

Keep faith, and trust in God that He will answer your prayer according to His will. He may not make the cancer go away or undo the accident, but He will provide comfort for your weary soul.

Date _____

_____

_____

_____

_____

_____

_____

_____

_____

_____

_____

_____

_____

_____

_____

_____

_____

_____

_____

_____

_____

My prayer for today _____

_____

_____

I cry aloud to the Lord; I lift up my voice to the Lord for mercy. I pour out my complaint before him; before him I tell my trouble. When my spirit grows faint within me, it is you who know my way. (Psalm 142:1–3)

A woman recently widowed said her wailing was so loud that she was sure it was greater than any wailing woman for hire. It's healthy to cry and wail, even scream. I would advise not to throw glass though. I did that once, and while it might have given me a momentary catharsis, the reality was I had a mess to clean up! Maybe a Nerf ball? Just a thought.

Date _____

_____

_____

_____

_____

_____

_____

_____

_____

_____

_____

_____

_____

_____

_____

_____

_____

_____

My prayer for today _____

_____

_____

Treasured Memory

My heart will be blessed with the sound of music and I'll sing once more.

—From *The Sound of Music* by Rodgers and Hammerstein

Martin Luther is quoted as saying, "He who sings to the Lord prays twice." Music is so powerful. Even if you are not a singer, turn up the music, and sing a joyful praise to the Lord! Singing is such sweet balm to the heart and soul. Write down your favorite hymn or Christian song, and sing along as you write.

Date _____

_____

_____

_____

_____

_____

_____

_____

_____

_____

_____

_____

_____

_____

_____

_____

_____

_____

My prayer for today _____

_____

_____

The salvation of the righteous comes from the Lord; he is their stronghold in time of trouble. (Psalm 37:39)

A stronghold is a place of security. Our God is our security and shelters us in our times of loneliness when we come to Him in prayer. In your loneliest of moments, trust that God is with you, and He is holding you in the palm of His hand.

Date _____

_____

_____

_____

_____

_____

_____

_____

_____

_____

_____

_____

_____

_____

_____

_____

_____

My prayer for today _____

_____

_____

Sing to God, sing praise to his name, extol him who rides on the clouds—his name is the Lord—and rejoice before him. A father to the fatherless, a defender of widows. (Psalm 68:4–5)

I think this verse says it all; praise God knowing that He loves you and has compassion for you. Trust in His love, and feel His peace.

Date _____

_____

_____

_____

_____

_____

_____

_____

_____

_____

_____

_____

_____

_____

_____

_____

_____

_____

_____

_____

_____

My prayer for today _____

_____

_____

I will say of the Lord, "He is my refuge and my fortress, my God, in whom I trust." (Psalm 91:2)

Trust and hope in the Lord bring strength. Waiting for a certain prayer to be answered on our terms takes away our strength. Trust in the Lord that His will be done. Trust His answer. Trust His timing in all things. He will renew your strength and make you whole again.

Date _____

_____

_____

_____

_____

_____

_____

_____

_____

_____

_____

_____

_____

_____

_____

_____

_____

_____

_____

_____

My prayer for today _____

_____

_____

For the Lord is good and his love endures forever; his faithfulness continues through all generations. (Psalm 100:5)

God's covenant with Abraham was that salvation would come through his lineage. They were both older at the time, and Sarah was past the childbearing years when an angel came to them and said they would have a son. But nothing is impossible to God, and our history in the Bible tells us they had a son, and our salvation did come through that lineage. God has a plan, but it is impossible for us to understand the mind of God. So don't try to understand His plan; strive to accept it and trust Him.

Date _____

_____

_____

_____

_____

_____

_____

_____

_____

_____

_____

_____

_____

_____

_____

_____

_____

_____

My prayer for today _____

_____

_____

I wait for the Lord, my soul waits, and in his word I put my hope. (Psalm 130:5)

In the quiet, lonely moments, open your Bible. Spend time in God's breathed Word, and let His words fill your soul.

Date _____

_____

_____

_____

_____

_____

_____

_____

_____

_____

_____

_____

_____

_____

_____

_____

_____

_____

_____

_____

My prayer for today _____

_____

_____

Let the morning bring me word of your unfailing love, for I have put my trust in you. Show me the way I should go, for to you I lift up my soul. (Psalm 143:8)

Begin each of your days in prayer. On days you don't know what to pray, trust that the Holy Spirit will intercede on your behalf, and God will listen to that prayer and continue to guide your path to healing.

Date _____

_____
_____
_____
_____
_____
_____
_____
_____
_____
_____
_____
_____
_____
_____
_____
_____
_____

My prayer for today _____
_____

But God made the earth by his power; he founded the world by his wisdom and stretched out the heavens by his understanding. (Jeremiah 10:12)

So profound! Think of the magnificence of our God. Ponder His creation and wonder in awe that you are a very special part of it. Words fail to describe His awesome power and His awesome love. With confidence we can know that He is in control and all powerful. Through Christ, your loved one is in a place where he or she knows a joy greater than you or I can possibly imagine. And one day you will know that joy as well.

Date _____

_____

_____

_____

_____

_____

_____

_____

_____

_____

_____

_____

_____

_____

_____

My prayer for today _____

_____

_____

Give thanks to the Lord Almighty, for the Lord is good; his love endures forever. (Jeremiah 33:11)

God is asking you to give thanks in spite of the pain you are in right now. Give thanks for having had the time you did with your loved one, for the memories you made, and for the hope you have in salvation.

Date _____

_____

_____

_____

_____

_____

_____

_____

_____

_____

_____

_____

_____

_____

_____

_____

_____

_____

_____

_____

My prayer for today _____

_____

_____

Simon Peter answered him, "Lord, to whom shall we go? You have the words of eternal life. We believe and know that you are the Holy One of God." (John 6:68)

God is real and promises us eternal life with Him. Christianity is the only faith where the Creator came into our world in the flesh in Jesus Christ, who testified to the truth and proved the reality of God to the world. Spend time in His Word, and be comforted by the promise of eternal life.

Date _____

_____

_____

_____

_____

_____

_____

_____

_____

_____

_____

_____

_____

_____

_____

_____

_____

_____

_____

My prayer for today _____

_____

_____

Write a letter to your loved one. Tell him or her about your day and how you feel. Or reminisce about a favorite memory.

Dear _____

For the message of the cross is foolishness to those who are perishing, but to us who are being saved it is the power of God. (1 Corinthians 1:18)

Christ was God manifested in human flesh so that we might see Him and believe! He conquered death, but before He ascended to heaven, He stayed in Jerusalem forty days, and many witnessed His resurrection. He removed all doubt that He is our risen Savior and proved that we have our hope in the cross. How great is our God, and how awesome is His power!

Date _____

_____

_____

_____

_____

_____

_____

_____

_____

_____

_____

_____

_____

_____

_____

_____

_____

My prayer for today _____

_____

_____

And now these three remain: faith, hope and love. But the greatest of these is love. (1 Corinthians 13:13)

Because God loves us so much, He sent His only Son to carry the burden of our sins to the cross so that we would have eternal life! Yes, the greatest of these is love!

Date _____

_____

_____

_____

_____

_____

_____

_____

_____

_____

_____

_____

_____

_____

_____

_____

_____

_____

_____

My prayer for today _____

_____

_____

Therefore we do not lose heart. Though outwardly we are wasting away, yet inwardly we are being renewed day by day. For our light and momentary troubles are achieving for us an eternal glory that far outweighs them all. So we fix our eyes not on what is seen, but on what is unseen. For what is seen is temporary, but what is unseen is eternal. (2 Corinthians 4:16–18)

There are times you may reflect on how unfair the death of your loved one is and focus on your grief. I remember being jealous when I would see people celebrating anniversaries or crying at the cards I would read in the Hallmark section. The thing is, when you are focused on your grief, it eclipses the joy that your loved one is experiencing now and will be yours one day. We all sit on the pity pot from time to time. The trick is to get off—and be sure to flush!

Date _____

_____

_____

_____

_____

_____

_____

_____

_____

_____

_____

_____

_____

_____

_____

My prayer for today _____

_____

_____

I have learned the secret of being content in any and every situation, whether well fed or hungry, whether living in plenty or in want. I can do everything through him who gives me strength. (Philippians 4:12–13)

No one can have immediate contentment in every situation, especially when someone we love dies. But we learn to cope with the loss over time. We become stronger, not of our own accord, but through our Father, who strengthens us.

Date _____

_____

_____

_____

_____

_____

_____

_____

_____

_____

_____

_____

_____

_____

_____

_____

_____

My prayer for today _____

_____

_____

Now may the Lord of peace himself give you peace at all times and in every way. The Lord be with all of you. The grace of our Lord Jesus Christ be with you all. (2 Thessalonians 3:16,18)

This is not to say that there won't be days with rain, but even in the midst of life's storms, I pray you have faith in all who God is and that you are filled with His peace.

Date _____

_____
_____
_____
_____
_____
_____
_____
_____
_____
_____
_____
_____
_____
_____
_____
_____
_____
_____
_____

My prayer for today _____
_____
_____

Let us fix our eyes on Jesus, the author and perfecter of our faith, who for the joy set before him endured the cross, scorning its shame, and sat down at the right hand of the throne of God. Consider him who endured such opposition from sinful men, so that you will not grow weary and lose heart. (Hebrews 12:2-3)

It is impossible for us to grasp the depth of love that God has for us and the tremendous burden of all our sins that Jesus carried to the cross so that we would have eternal life. Yes, we have pain in this world, but take heart. The best is yet to come.

Date _____

_____

_____

_____

_____

_____

_____

_____

_____

_____

_____

_____

_____

_____

_____

_____

_____

_____

My prayer for today _____

_____

_____

You have heard of Job's perseverance and have seen what the Lord finally brought about. The Lord is full of compassion and mercy. (James 5:11)

My husband was diagnosed with ALS at age thirty-seven. He was so young, and we were devastated. Three years after the diagnosis, he was now in a wheelchair, and our house burned to the ground. There was nothing left. We were in shock at how unfair life seemed. In time I began to see God's work in the ashes. The miracle was to give my husband purpose again. Being confined to the wheelchair, he was forced to watch me go to work every day to keep our insurance. Our children had to feed him, and either I or the nurse would have to bathe him. But now he had a house to build. He created the blueprint, oversaw the construction, and put a roof over our heads. I am so thankful to God for giving him that most perfect purpose. Try to see the purpose in your circumstance, and may God manifest His glory in you.

Date _____

_____

_____

_____

_____

_____

_____

_____

_____

_____

_____

_____

_____

_____

_____

My prayer for today _____

_____

_____

Then Jesus told him [Thomas], "Because you have seen me, you have believed; blessed are those who have not seen and yet have believed. (John 20:29)

When I was six years old, I was playing with my cousin one beautiful summer day. There were just a few popcorn clouds set against a perfectly blue sky. In all my childish wisdom I was telling her that when it storms with thunder and lightning, God is angry. But when it is a soft, gentle rain, He is sad, and those are heaven's tears. She looked up to the sky and asked, "Is that true, God?" Suddenly, three very white clouds appeared in the blue sky: Y-E-S. As an adult, I don't believe all weather patterns reflect God's temperament, but I've always been grateful that He took the time to speak to two little girls on that summer day so long ago. In times of great trial and doubt in my life, I remember that moment. I have seen, and I believe! In what way has God revealed Himself to you?

Date _____

_____

_____

_____

_____

_____

_____

_____

_____

_____

_____

_____

_____

_____

_____

My prayer for today _____

_____

_____

Tired cloud lets go
Raindrop falls to pond below
Ripple continues on

I wrote this haiku after my husband died. He was so tired from his long illness and finally surrendered to death. But I knew that he had affected so many people in such a positive way. I was the person I came to be in part because of him. It was important to me to honor his memory by living my life joyfully and not in sorrow or bitterness. What would your loved one wish for you?

Date _____

_____

_____

_____

_____

_____

_____

_____

_____

_____

_____

_____

_____

_____

_____

_____

_____

My prayer for today _____

_____

_____

Shall we accept good from God, and not trouble? (Job 2:10)

Try to focus for a moment each day on your blessings. Having an attitude of thankfulness puts things in perspective. I hate that my husband died at such a young age, but I am deeply thankful God blessed us with the years we did have together and the memories we made. Strive to find the good He gives, and give thanks. What are you thankful for today?

Date _____

_____

_____

_____

_____

_____

_____

_____

_____

_____

_____

_____

_____

_____

_____

_____

_____

_____

_____

My prayer for today _____

_____

_____

Treasured Memory

O Lord my God, I take refuge in you. (Psalm 7:1)

What you surround yourself with shapes who you are. Surround yourself in God's glory by reading His Word, going to church, and listening to Christian music. Find peace in the timelessness of God.

Date _____

_____

_____

_____

_____

_____

_____

_____

_____

_____

_____

_____

_____

_____

_____

_____

_____

_____

_____

_____

My prayer for today _____

_____

_____

O Lord, our Lord, how majestic is your name in all the earth! When I consider your heavens, the work of your fingers, the moon and the stars, which you have set in place, what is man that you are mindful of him, the son of man that you care for him? You made him a little lower than the heavenly beings and crowned him with glory and honor. (Psalm 8: 1, 3–5)

I love these verses! Take comfort as you ponder all that God has created. It's amazing that our God, who created the heavens and the earth and all that is in it, is mindful of us and that He loves us so much He sent His Son to die on the cross for our salvation.

Date _____

_____

_____

_____

_____

_____

_____

_____

_____

_____

_____

_____

_____

_____

_____

_____

My prayer for today _____

_____

_____

God is our refuge and strength, an ever-present help in trouble. Therefore we will not fear, though the earth give way and the mountains fall into the heart of the sea. (Psalm 46:1–2)

Whether suddenly due to an accident or over time due to a long illness, the truth is your loved one's death has forever changed your world. Trust in God, my friend, He holds your world in the palm of His hand.

Date _____

_____

_____

_____

_____

_____

_____

_____

_____

_____

_____

_____

_____

_____

_____

_____

_____

My prayer for today _____

_____

_____

Create in me a pure heart, O God, and renew a steadfast spirit within me. Do not cast me from your presence or take your Holy Spirit from me. Restore to me the joy of your salvation and grant me a willing spirit to sustain me. (Psalm 51:10–12)

The key words in this scripture are "a willing spirit to sustain me." My prayer is for you to have a willing spirit that seeks the joy in each day, even when some days you may have to look a little harder.

Date _____

_____

_____

_____

_____

_____

_____

_____

_____

_____

_____

_____

_____

_____

_____

_____

_____

_____

My prayer for today _____

_____

_____

I call as my heart grows faint; lead me to the rock that is higher than I. For you have been my refuge. (Psalm 61:2–3)

God is our strength in times of trial. Pain is not something we ask for, but the scars left from the pain serve as great reminders of how much we've matured in Christ. There is no growth without the rain. We find our joy in the hope we have in Christ amidst our suffering.

Date _____

_____

_____

_____

_____

_____

_____

_____

_____

_____

_____

_____

_____

_____

_____

_____

_____

_____

_____

My prayer for today _____

_____

_____

Your word is a lamp to my feet and a light for my path. (Psalm 119:105)

Be in God's Word; read the Bible, and use it to guide your path. When I was young, I was told to treat the Bible as something very fragile and to take great care when handling it. To write or mark in it was greatly frowned on. Dear friend, the Bible is not fragile. God's Word is not fragile. Read your Bible, and take a marker to highlight the verses that speak to you. Put notes in the margins, and know that God is revealing Himself to you.

Date _____

_____

_____

_____

_____

_____

_____

_____

_____

_____

_____

_____

_____

_____

_____

_____

_____

_____

_____

My prayer for today _____

_____

_____

But for you who revere my name, the sun of righteousness will rise with healing in its wings. (Malachi 4:2)

I love sunrises. One of my favorite Ziggy cartoons by Tom Wilson consisted of one cel of Ziggy sitting on a hillside watching the sunrise, clapping his hands, and exclaiming, "Go God!" As sure as the sun rises each day, my friend, God is with you and will never forsake you.

Date _____

_____
_____
_____
_____
_____
_____
_____
_____
_____
_____
_____
_____
_____
_____
_____
_____
_____
_____

My prayer for today _____

_____
_____

For God so loved the world that he gave his one and only Son, that whoever believes in him shall not perish but have eternal life. (John 3:16)

Here in lies our hope! Your time in this life is forever changed; you are left behind to carry on, to raise the kids, play with the grandchildren, to do the chores, and pay the bills. But you have this promise: This is not your final destination. Nor was it for your loved one.

Date _____

_____

_____

_____

_____

_____

_____

_____

_____

_____

_____

_____

_____

_____

_____

_____

My prayer for today _____

_____

_____

Lovely desert flower
Blooms amid adversity
Joy in suffering

Over time my anguish and fatigue began to lessen, and my gratefulness for the time I had with my husband began to emerge. I am so grateful for the years we had together and for the memories we were able to share. I wrote this haiku in the dawning of my restoration. It is in the promise of salvation that we find our joy in suffering. I pray you, like the desert flower, are blooming amid your pain.

Date _____

_____

_____

_____

_____

_____

_____

_____

_____

_____

_____

_____

_____

_____

_____

_____

_____

My prayer for today _____

_____

_____

By the word of the Lord were the heavens made, their starry host by the breath of his mouth. (Psalm 33:6)

Really ponder this verse. How great and awesome is our God! And how awesome is He that He loves us and listens when we call His name! Journal your thankfulness and praise to the Lord.

Date _____

_____

_____

_____

_____

_____

_____

_____

_____

_____

_____

_____

_____

_____

_____

_____

_____

_____

My prayer for today _____

_____

_____

Write a letter to your loved one. Tell him or her about your day and how you feel. Or reminisce about a favorite memory.

Dear _____

Better is one day in your courts than a thousand elsewhere. (Psalm 84:10)

Creating this journal has been a difficult time of reliving my personal journey of grief. A friend suggested I read a psalm each time before I start writing. The first time I did I turned to this psalm; the song lyrics, "better is one day in your court than a thousand elsewhere," had been continually playing in my mind for days prior! I love the moments God opens our eyes to His voice. God is speaking. Are you listening?

Date _____

_____

_____

_____

_____

_____

_____

_____

_____

_____

_____

_____

_____

_____

_____

_____

My prayer for today _____

_____

_____

Before the mountains were born or you brought forth the earth and the world, from everlasting to everlasting you are God. (Psalm 90:2)

I find this verse so comforting as it reminds me of God's awesomeness. He created the world, the universe, and the heavens above. Our God is the beginning and the end of time, which is represented in the tapers of each page break in this journal symbolizing eternity past and eternity future. In Him we have unwavering confidence that He is in control, and His promise of salvation truly is ours.

Date _____

_____

_____

_____

_____

_____

_____

_____

_____

_____

_____

_____

_____

_____

_____

My prayer for today _____

_____

_____

And we rejoice in the hope of the glory of God. Not only so, but we also rejoice in our sufferings, because we know that suffering produces perseverance; perseverance, character; and character, hope. And hope does not disappoint us, because God has poured out his love into our hearts by the Holy Spirit, whom he has given us. (Romans 5:2–3)

I believe suffering forces us to realize our complete dependence on Christ. Look to the Lord for strength in the moment with your hope in salvation. This complete surrender grows us in our relationship with Jesus, and we are renewed in spirit.

Date _____

_____

_____

_____

_____

_____

_____

_____

_____

_____

_____

_____

_____

_____

_____

_____

My prayer for today _____

_____

_____

Being confident of this, that he who began a good work in you will carry it on to completion until the day of Christ Jesus. (Philippians 1:6)

I stand in awe as I contemplate this verse. God began a good work in me? That's an incredible thing to ponder. God loves you so much, and He has begun a good work in you. Can you imagine? And He will carry it on to completion. You have a very bright future!

Date _____

_____

_____

_____

_____

_____

_____

_____

_____

_____

_____

_____

_____

_____

_____

_____

_____

_____

My prayer for today _____

_____

_____

All the days ordained for me were written in your book before one of them came to be. (Psalm 139:16)

I find such comfort in this verse. God is in control. He has ordained our seasons; the painful storms are not to be cruel but to grow us to know His heart, to call on Him to be our Father, and for us to be His children. We live in a fallen world, and while we live here for a time, we have hope in our future, and we learn to trust God's perfect timing in all things.

Date _____

_____

_____

_____

_____

_____

_____

_____

_____

_____

_____

_____

_____

_____

_____

_____

_____

_____

My prayer for today _____

_____

_____

Finally, brothers and sisters, rejoice! Strive for full restoration, encourage one another, be of one mind, live in peace. And the God of love and peace will be with you. (2 Corinthians 13:11)

During the time my husband was in the end stages of ALS, a teenager was killed in a tragic accident. He was seventeen, and the grief was unbearable for his mother. We attended the same church, and our pastor asked us to meet and share our grief with each other. It really was helpful to both of us to share our pain and encourage each other. Is there a person who needs encouraging in your life?

Date _____

_____

_____

_____

_____

_____

_____

_____

_____

_____

_____

_____

_____

_____

_____

_____

_____

My prayer for today _____

_____

_____

There is a time for everything and a season for every activity under heaven. A time to weep and a time to laugh; a time to mourn and a time to dance. (Ecclesiastes 3:1, 4)

Give yourself permission to laugh, dance, and be joyful. By living life joyfully you encourage others to trust that God's love and compassion will give them the strength needed to endure their grief. Manifest God's glory through witnessing to others and choosing to live life abundantly.

Date _____

_____

_____

_____

_____

_____

_____

_____

_____

_____

_____

_____

_____

_____

_____

_____

_____

_____

My prayer for today _____

_____

_____

Love is patient, love is kind. It does not envy, it does not boast, it is not proud. It is not rude, it is not self-seeking, it is not easily angered, it keeps no record of wrongs. Love does not delight in evil but rejoices with the truth. It always protects, always trusts, always hopes, always perseveres. Love never fails. (1 Corinthians 13:4–8)

Our God is love. He is the very source of love. We were created in His image, and it is only through Him that we are capable of love. Be thankful to the Lord for the blessing of love and for the special person with whom you were able to share that love.

Date _____

_____

_____

_____

_____

_____

_____

_____

_____

_____

_____

_____

_____

_____

_____

My prayer for today _____

_____

_____

Treasured Memory

Those who sow in tears will reap with songs of joy. He who goes out weeping, carrying seed to sow, will return with songs of joy, carrying sheaves with him. (Psalm 126:5–6)

The season of grief is just that—a season. As you progress through the stages of grief, there is light at the end of the tunnel; there is joy once again. Welcome the joy. This is not a sign of moving on. You are honoring your loved one's memory by living a joyful life.

Date _____

_____

_____

_____

_____

_____

_____

_____

_____

_____

_____

_____

_____

_____

_____

_____

_____

My prayer for today _____

_____

_____

Blessed are you who hunger now, for you will be satisfied. Blessed are you who weep now, for you will laugh. (Luke 6:21)

You will never forget your loved one. But over time, you will learn to laugh again while remaining grateful for the memories. Pray for God to help you stop loving the past so much that you aren't capable of living in the present and living each moment, as your loved one would have wanted you to—joyfully.

Date _____

_____

_____

_____

_____

_____

_____

_____

_____

_____

_____

_____

_____

_____

_____

_____

_____

_____

My prayer for today _____

_____

_____

For everything that was written in the past was written to teach us, so that through endurance and the encouragement of the Scriptures we might have hope. (Romans 15:4)

When you read through the Scriptures, it is evident how Providence is woven throughout history. Seeing God's hand at work in His creation gives us confidence in His promises. One of the nice things about journaling is that you have your own record now of how God has been at work in your life. I pray you see the good work God has done in you, and you have learned to live joyfully in the Spirit.

Date _____

_____

_____

_____

_____

_____

_____

_____

_____

_____

_____

_____

_____

_____

_____

_____

_____

My prayer for today _____

_____

_____

May the God of hope fill you with all joy and peace as you trust in him, so that you may overflow with hope by the power of the Holy Spirit. (Romans 15:13)

There is so much pain and suffering in this world. As you've progressed on your journey, do you see a time when you may be able to reach out to others who have recently experienced loss? Helping others brings joy to ourselves because we are doing God's work in demonstrating His love and compassion for all His children.

Date _____

_____

_____

_____

_____

_____

_____

_____

_____

_____

_____

_____

_____

_____

_____

_____

_____

_____

_____

My prayer for today _____

_____

_____

Be at rest once more, O my soul, for the Lord has been good to you. For you, O Lord, have delivered my soul from death, my eyes from tears, my feet from stumbling, that I may walk before the Lord in the land of the living. (Psalm 116:7–9)

The journey of grief is the most difficult journey we as humans will take. We love, and therefore we risk the pain of losing that love. When you are able to look back on your journey and with a grateful heart give thanks to the Lord for the blessing of the love you shared, you can once again live life joyfully and abundantly. May God manifest His glory through you as you shine His light so brilliantly it cannot be ignored.

Date _____

_____

_____

_____

_____

_____

_____

_____

_____

_____

_____

_____

_____

_____

_____

_____

My prayer for today _____

_____

_____

Praise be to the God and Father of our Lord Jesus Christ, the Father of compassion and the God of all comfort, who comforts us in all our troubles, so that we can comfort those in any trouble with the comfort we ourselves have received from God. For just as the sufferings of Christ flow over into our lives, so also through Christ our comfort overflows. (2 Corinthians 1:3–5)

Your journey doesn't really end, but it does take a new direction. You've been on this journey for some time now, and you've learned things about yourself through this experience. Can you find it within yourself to reach out to others who are suffering so that you can comfort others through Christ who comforts you?

Date _____

_____

_____

_____

_____

_____

_____

_____

_____

_____

_____

_____

_____

_____

_____

_____

_____

My prayer for today _____

_____

_____

And I heard a loud voice from the throne saying, "Now the dwelling of God is with men, and he will live with them. They will be his people, and God himself will be with them and be their God. He will wipe every tear from their eyes. There will be no more death or mourning or crying or pain, for the old order of things has passed away. (Revelation 21:3–4)

Amen! Come, Lord Jesus!

Date _____

_____

_____

_____

_____

_____

_____

_____

_____

_____

_____

_____

_____

_____

_____

_____

_____

_____

My prayer for today _____

_____

_____

CPSIA information can be obtained
at www.ICGtesting.com
Printed in the USA
LVHW091901050322
712717LV00002B/9